BOBBIE LORD

Reflections

A Journal for Women to Discover Healing and Purpose

Seascapes Press

Reflections: A Journal for Women to
Discover Healing and Purpose

ISBN 979-8-9856024-2-5

Cover design by Aaxel Author Services & Natasha D'Costa
Interior design by Aaxel Author Services

Cover photo: Zambezi River, Zambia by Bobbie Lord

Printed in the United States of America

"It is the recognition of the sacred in daily life – a deep gratitude for the wonders of the world and the delicate web of interconnectedness between people, nature and things – recognition that true intimacy based on respect and love is a measure of a life well lived."

- Joan Borysenko, *A Woman's Book of Life*

Introduction

What does it mean, to reflect? To reflect is to think deeply or carefully about something. Likewise, refection involves giving serious thought or consideration to something. For the cover for this journal, I chose a photo I took while on a safari on the Lower Zambezi River in Zambia. As we returned to camp from a sundowner of cocktails and hors d'oeuvres, our banana boat capsized when, suddenly, a hippo surfaced under the bow, and crocodiles lined the opposite bank. The film survived, but my camera didn't. Later, at dinner, which involved many glasses of wine, everyone reflected on how fortunate we were when rescued by another banana boat, without harm from the hippo or the crocodiles.

In 1999, I worked at the Qatrom Refugee Camp as part of a humanitarian mission. It was the Kosovar refugees who inspired me to write this journal. After witnessing their pain and suffering, I pondered the best way to aid them in their recovery from their trauma. I knew journaling could be a means of healing, so I researched journaling for four months before writing *Reflections*.

What you have in your hand is not just a journal for refugees, but for anyone compelled to explore universal truths and to think deeply about what is essential for a full, rich life.

My hope is that this journal facilitates your journey through a peaceful and mindful life.

Gratitude

Over the next 7 days, list everything you are grateful for (for example: loved ones, country, traditions, friends, food, nature, blessings, etc.) Acknowledge with gratitude what you have done each day.

Overcoming Fear

What emotions do you need to feel (for example: anger, resentment, pain, sorrow, hate, fear, etc.)? Write until you feel those emotions.

"The freedom of feeling every emotion we have, without denial, allows us to access the sacred and empowering gifts of choice and free will."

- Jamie Sams, *Earth Medicine*

How have you overcome fear?

What lessons have you learned in overcoming your challenges?

How would your life be different if you felt safe to share your thoughts and feelings, and knew you were heard and accepted?

Grief

What tears do you need to shed? Allow yourself to shed tears, to cry out in pain and sorrow, to grieve.

What loved ones have you lost? How have you said goodbye? What rituals have you used? List the things you most admire and remember about that person. Incorporate those characteristics into yourself.

How can sharing your suffering and pain, darkness, anger, fear and alienation help others?

Community

How have your friends helped you cope with change?

How have you helped your friends?

How can you stay connected to your family, traditions, culture?

What personal stories and memories of your Elders have influenced you?

What can you pass on to the next generation?

List the ways through which to create respect, trust, intimacy and unity within all your relationships.

Compassion

How have others shown compassion towards you?
How do you allow others to help you?

What do you do to be compassionate?

Nourishing the Soul

Nurture means to nourish. Women are natural nurturers. They know how to nurture others. Now we must find ways to care for the self. Self-nurturing restores and refreshes. It is calming and energizing, loving and kind. List the ways in which you are kind and gentle with yourself.

What inspires you, nurtures you and gives you a sense of fulfillment?

How is love being nurtured in your heart today?

List simple pleasures you love (for example, watching a sunset, being in nature, eating comfort foods, etc.).

List smells, sounds and tastes of things that were good in your childhood.

What music soothes you, inspires you, makes you feel good? How often do you listen to music?

List the ways through which you listen to your inner voice of wisdom.

Laughter

Laughter is food for the soul. Humor brings balance
and lightness into our lives. What makes you laugh?

What brings a tender smile to your lips?

What makes you laugh so hard that tears stream down your face? How long has it been since you laughed like that? Who in your childhood made you laugh?

What mistakes have you made that you can laugh about?

Forgiveness

Forgiveness can bring peace of mind and heal pain. Forgiveness does not condone abuse, violence, aggression or betrayal. Anger and resentfulness cannot be denied or ignored if genuine forgiveness is achieved. What does forgiveness mean to you?

"*[Forgiveness] is a decision, an attitude, a process and a way of life. Forgiveness is a decision to see beyond fears, idiosyncrasies, neuroses and mistakes...*"

- Robin Casajian, *Forgiveness, A Bold Choice for a Peaceful Heart*

What are the challenges of forgiveness? What should be forgiven?

Why should you forgive?

How can you heal through forgiveness?

How do you forgive?

What and whom do you need to forgive?

Being a Woman

As a woman, reflect on lost worlds or freedoms gained.

What connects women everywhere?

"Flowers teach us that every color and shape is individual and beautiful. They teach their human counterparts to love the differences in shape and form without comparing the beauty of one over the other."

- Jamie Sams, *Earth Medicine*

What do women have in common?

What kind of initiation into womanhood did you experience? How will you introduce your daughters to womanhood?

How did men (father, brothers, uncles, grandfathers) treat you as a female? How would you want it to have been different?

How do you want your daughters to be treated as women?

How do you want your sons to treat women?

How would it be if a group of women came together
to talk and to share?

How can we, as women, bring peace into the world?

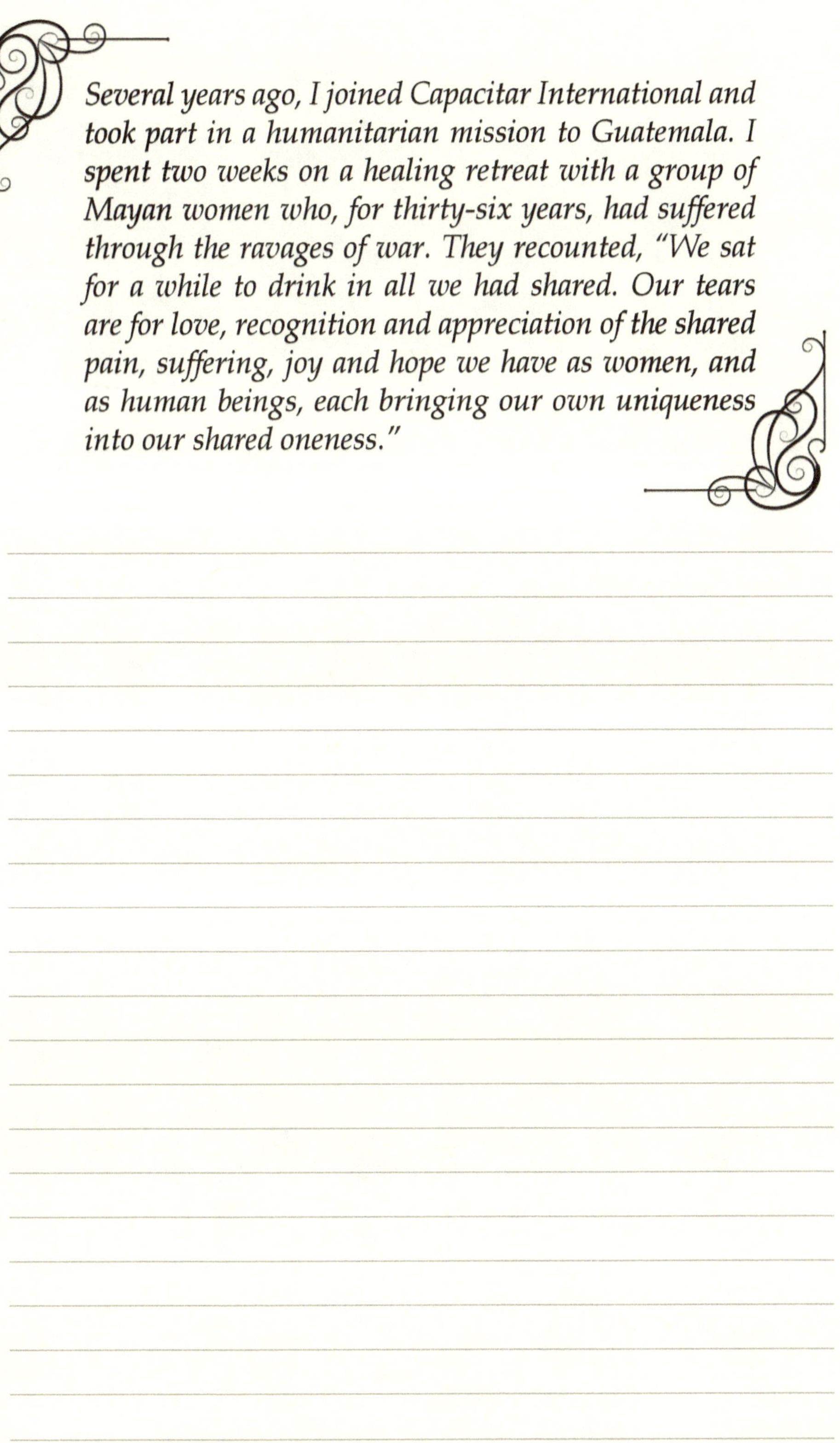

Several years ago, I joined Capacitar International and took part in a humanitarian mission to Guatemala. I spent two weeks on a healing retreat with a group of Mayan women who, for thirty-six years, had suffered through the ravages of war. They recounted, "We sat for a while to drink in all we had shared. Our tears are for love, recognition and appreciation of the shared pain, suffering, joy and hope we have as women, and as human beings, each bringing our own uniqueness into our shared oneness."

Conclusion

My purpose for writing a guided journal was to help women recover from trauma and to discover their strength and resilience. In the process, I discovered my strength and understood, on a deeper level, how interconnected we are. I hope this journaling experience will assist in your growth and understanding.

— Bobbie

Roberta (Bobbie) Lord spent eleven years working overseas in the humanitarian field, where her focus was working with refugees in Kenya, Albania, Kosovo, and Guatemala as well as village men and women in Zambia. With Relief International under the umbrella of UNCHR, she served as camp manager at the Qatrom Refugee Camp in Albania, where the refugees nicknamed her "Mother of the Camp."

Bobbie also facilitated workshops in the United States, including at Princess Basma Centre for Disabled Children in Jerusalem, where she developed a program for the mothers of disabled children, and at Interfaith Refugee and Immigration Ministries in Chicago, where she assisted resettled refugee and immigrant women in improving their lives through social and economic development. She also has been a guest lecturer to many organizations including various women's clubs, Rotary Clubs, and church groups.

No longer working overseas, she continues to empower young women while working as a house director in sororities on university campuses.

Bobbie considers herself foremost a humanitarian supporting those who have no voice. Reflections was inspired by her work with refugee women. She is also the author of *Without a Homeland*, based on her work at the Qatrom Refugee Camp. She has two sons, six grandchildren and two great-grandchildren. She can be reached at www.bobbielord.com.